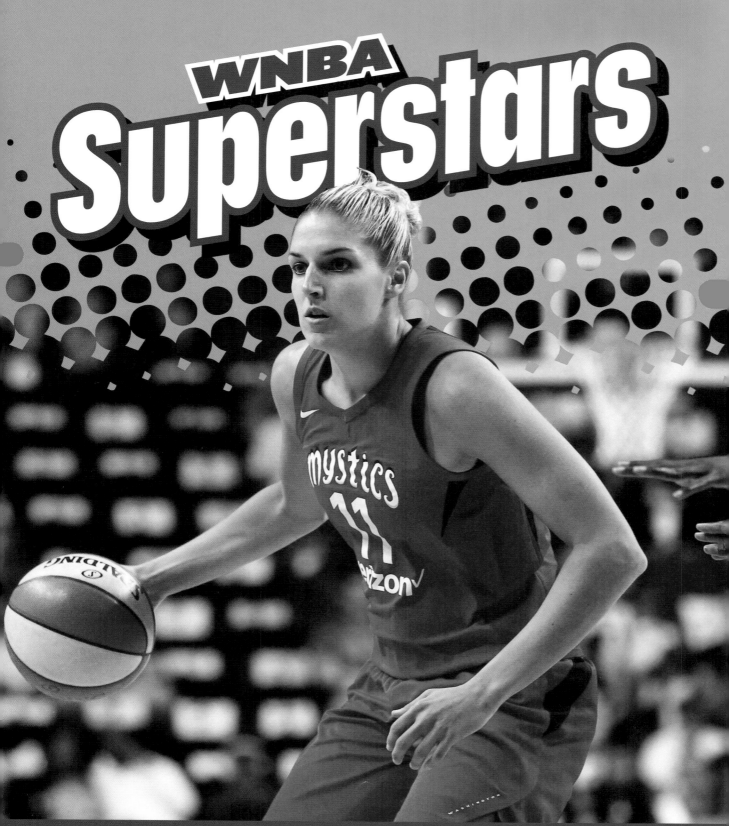

WNBA Superstars

BY K.C. KELLEY

Elena Delle Donne ▶

The Child's World®
childsworld.com

Published by The Child's World®
1980 Lookout Drive • Mankato, MN 56003-1705
800-599-READ • www.childsworld.com

Photographs:
Cover: Jennifer Buchanan/USA Today Sports/Imagn.
AP Images: Elaine Thompson 5, 17; John Amis 9,
Ralph Freso 18. Newscom: Rich von Biberstein/Icon
SW 2; Jeffrey Brown/Icon SW 6; Quinn Harris/Icon
SW 10; David Dennis/Icon SW 13; Mingo Nesmith/
Icon SW 14; Chuck Myers/MCT.

ISBN 9781503835337
LCCN 2019944746

Printed in the United States of America

Contents

Hardwood Heroes

Fans pack the **arena** to cheer for their favorite stars. The action on the wooden court is fierce and exciting. What's the game? It's basketball! The Women's National Basketball Association (WNBA) features the best players in the world. Twelve teams play each summer to see who will be the league champion. Those teams are led by the superstars in this book. Let's meet the very best of today's WNBA!

Superstar vs. Superstar: Breanna Stewart tries to dribble around Brittney Griner. ▶

Liz Cambage

Australian hero Liz Cambage took a while to be a WNBA star. Cambage played the 2011 and 2013 WNBA seasons in Tulsa. Then she played several seasons in China and Australia. She returned to play for the WNBA's Dallas Wings in 2018. Cambage made the WNBA All-Star team that season. She also set a WNBA single-game record with 53 points! In 2019, she joined the Las Vegas Aces.

Team: Las Vegas Aces

Height: 6'8" (2.0 m)

Position: Center

College: None (Australia)

Joined WNBA: 2011

Cambage is tall and strong. She can reach over defenders to score.

Skylar Diggins-Smith

In 2018, Skylar Diggins-Smith made her third All-WNBA team. She uses all-around skills to lead her team to wins. Few players are able to both score and pass as well as she can. Playing guard, she has to be creative to make passes. She has to be fierce to **drive** to the basket. Diggins-Smith can do it all!

Team: Dallas Wings
Height: 5'9" (1.75 m)
Position: Guard
College: Notre Dame
Joined WNBA: 2013

As the point guard, Diggins-Smith tells teammates what plays to run. ▶

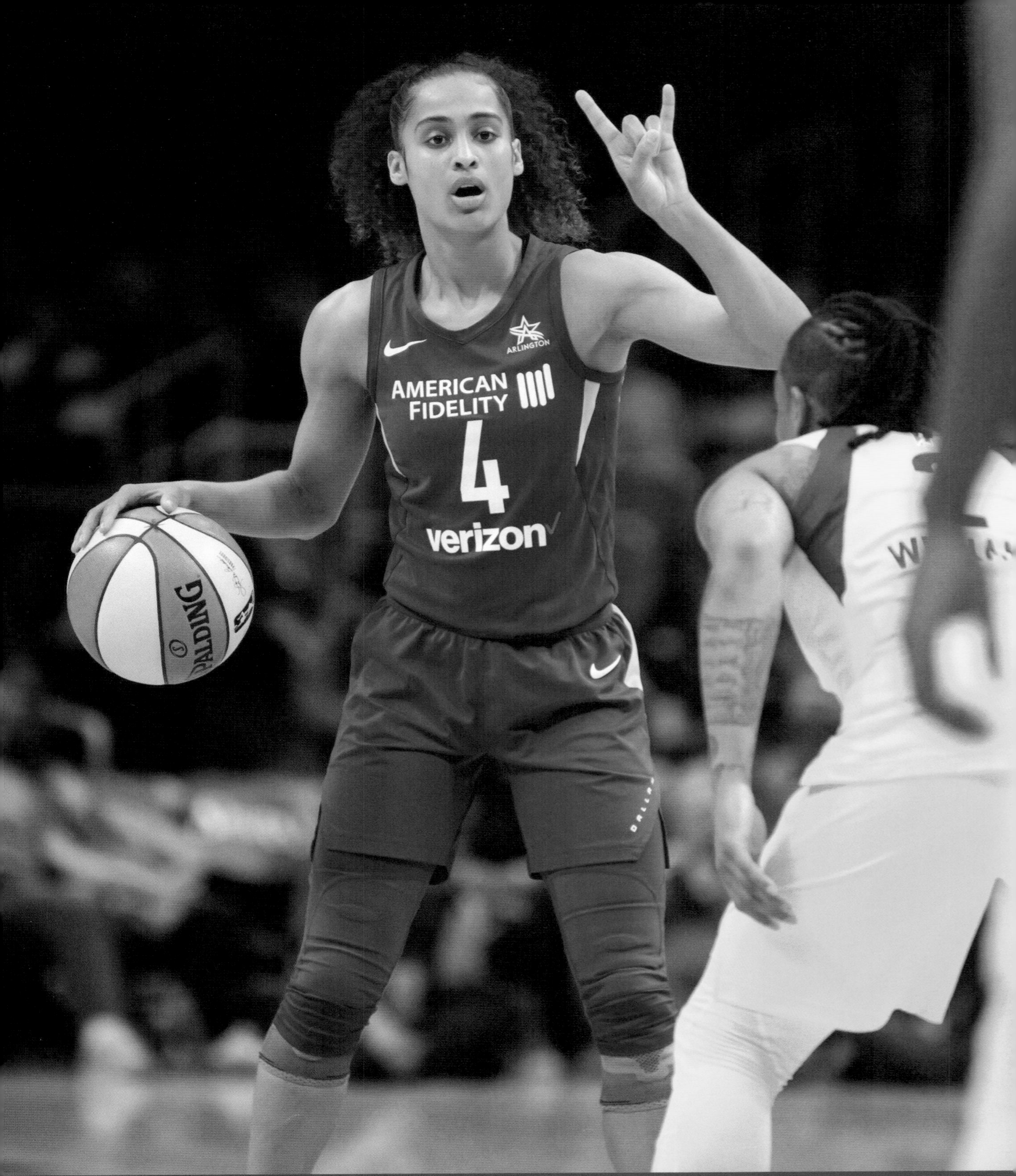
AMERICAN
FIDELITY
4
verizon
ARLINGTON
SPALDING

Elena Delle Donne

In college, Elena Delle Donne led the nation in scoring. She has continued to pour in points in the WNBA. In 2013, she was **Rookie** of the Year and a WNBA All-Star. In 2015, she was the WNBA MVP! The next year, the Washington Mystics star tied for the league scoring lead. Delle Donne's height and smooth moves make her very hard to stop!

Team: Washington Mystics

Height: 6'5" (1.95 m)

Position: Forward

College: Delaware

Joined WNBA: 2013

Some tall players do not dribble well. That's not the case with all-around star Delle Donne. ▶

Brittney Griner

Don't try to get a shot past Brittney Griner. She's probably going to block it! This five-time All-Star is one of the best shot-blockers ever. In fact, she has the third-most blocks in WNBA history. Griner is also one of the WNBA's top **rebounders**. Plus, she has 10 regular-season **dunks**—that's more than the rest of the WNBA combined! Griner's trophy case includes a 2014 WNBA championship trophy and a 2016 Olympic gold medal!

Team: Phoenix Mercury

Height: 6'9" (2.06 m)

Position: Center

College: Baylor

Joined WNBA: 2013

Griner is great on defense, but she can attack the basket to score, too.

Candace Parker

Candace Parker needs a whole room for all her trophies. She has won two WNBA MVP awards. She led the Sparks to the 2016 WNBA title. She has been on five All-WNBA first teams (and three second teams!). Don't forget her 2008 Rookie of the Year trophy and her two Olympic gold medals! At Tennessee, she was the national player of the year twice. Parker's all-around game and scoring skills helped her earn all that **hardware**!

Team: Los Angeles Sparks

Height: 6'4" (1.93 m)

Position: Forward

College: Tennessee

Joined WNBA: 2008

When Parker and the Sparks won the WBA title, she was the WNBA Finals MVP.

Breanna Stewart

This superstar is used to winning! Stewart's UConn teams won 151 games in four years—and lost only 5! She was the first college player ever named tops in the country three times. With the Storm, she has kept winning! Stewart reached 1,000 career points faster than any other WNBA player. In 2018, Stewart led the Storm to the WNBA title. She was named the **regular-season** and WNBA Finals MVP!

Team: Seattle Storm
Height: 6'4" (1.93 m)
Position: Forward
College: Connecticut
Joined WNBA: 2016

Stewart scored at least 600 points in each of her first three seasons in Seattle.

Diana Taurasi

Diana Taurasi is the WNBA's all-time leading scorer. You can't get better than that! The high-scoring guard can put in points from the inside, outside, and everywhere in between. She also holds the WNBA record for **three-point field goals**. Taurasi plays harder than any other player in the league. She was the number one overall pick by Phoenix in the 2004 **draft**. Since then she has led Phoenix to three titles (2007, 2009, 2014).

Team: Phoenix Mercury

Height: 6'0" (1.83 m)

Position: Guard

College: Connecticut

Joined WNBA: 2004

Taurasi has been named to the All-WNBA First Team 10 times. That's the most ever.

Courtney Vandersloot

Many stars score a lot of points. Someone has to get them the ball, though. Courtney Vandersloot is one of the WNBA's best all-time passers. She holds Chicago career and single-season records for **assists**. In 2018, she really got to work. Her 258 assists set a new WNBA record. Vandersloot keeps busy when the WNBA is not playing. She has played in Turkey, Croatia, Poland, and Hungary.

Team: Chicago

Height: 5'8" (1.73 m)

Position: Guard

College: Gonzaga

Joined WNBA: 2011

Vandersloot is not afraid to push past taller players on her way to the basket. ▶

Glossary

arena (un-REE-nuh) the large building in which basketball teams play

assists (uh-SISTS) passes that lead directly to baskets

draft (DRAFT) the annual event at which new WNBA players are chosen from college teams

drive (DRYVE) to dribble toward the basket past defenders to try to score

dunks (DUNX) shots that are slammed directly into the hoop

hardware (HARD-ware) nickname for sports trophies and medals won by athletes

rebounder (REE-bownd-er) a player who grabs shots that miss the basket

regular season (REG-you-lur SEEZ-un) the part of a sports calendar before the playoffs begin

rookie (RUH-kee) a player in her first year of a pro sport

three-point field goals (THREE-POYNT FEELD GOHLZ) baskets that are made from behind an arc on the floor

Find Out More

IN THE LIBRARY

Delle Donne, Elena. *Full-Court Press*.
New York, NY: Harper Entertainment, 2018.
(Note: This is a novel by the Washington Mystics' star player.)

Levit, Joe. *Basketball's G.O.A.T.: Michael Jordan,
LeBron James, and More (Sports' Greatest of All
Time)*. New York, NY: Lerner Publishing, 2019.

Sports Illustrated Kids. *My First Book of Basketball*.
New York, NY: Sports Illustrated Kids, 2018.

ON THE WEB

Visit our Web site for links about the
WNBA's superstars:
childsworld.com/links

Note to Parents, Teachers, and Librarians:
We routinely verify our Web links to make sure they are safe
and active sites. So encourage your readers to check them out!

Index

About the Author

K.C. Kelley is the author of more than 100 books on sports for young readers, as well as many sports biographies. He lives in Santa Barbara, California.